GREEN REGALIA

poems by

Adam Tavel

STEPHEN F. AUSTIN STATE UNIVERSITY PRESS

For more information:
Stephen F. Austin State University Press
P.O. Box 13007 SFA Station
Nacogdoches, Texas 75962
sfapress@sfasu.edu
www.sfasu.edu/sfapress

Managing Editor: Kimberly Verhines
Book design: Katt Noble
Cover Art: Madara Mason

Distributed by Texas A&M Consortium
www.tamupress.com

ISBN: 978-1-62288-232-8

for
William Hathaway

We are both in a world
Where the dirt is God.
    -Ted Hughes

Contents

~

I

II

III

IV

I

How to Write a Nature Poem

Begin with a tedious parade
of details, like how the mucus
squid picks a cave to spray
its eggs, or how the discovery
of cartilage in dodo knees
changes their presumptive diet
to the following kinds
of berries. Assume readers
enjoy being trapped
in the merlot-breath lecture
of a stranger's uncle, blocking
the bathroom door. Obsess
over color, being sure to name
your fancy crayons: carmine,
cornsilk, papayawhip.
If a person appears, make her
your daughter, resplendent
in a sundress, a symbol
for the awe we all need
to find in order to survive
the fourth stanza.
Remember the menace
of power lines, logging trucks,
uncut plastic ringlets
from a six-pack swirling
in the marsh. It should end
with an image of affirmed
endurance, like an interstate
where haggard drivers brake
until a gaggle of goslings

waddle safely from the road.
Make sure their mother
is dead. Make sure the runt
lags behind but catches up.

Bloom

We must not call them ghosts

          film's pulsing jellyfish

their thousand crowded palms

          a thousand paupers thinned

or floating burst balloons

          papyral skins that skim

translucent so the sea

          can color them with waves

we must not think the soul

          returns like this a bloom

in opaque light removed

          from fear it reaches here

with poisoned tentacles

          the tiny gills stunned still

as when a father slaps

          his toddler's face the fish

drawn in and liquified

          its wobbly eyes unroot

scales shucked and cast into

          the blue a fathomed bruise

Vigil

The summer that my father left I drowned
my snuggle lamb inside our kiddie pool
to watch it bloat. My audience of bees
labored and spun among the buttercups
grandmother no longer mowed herself.
I too took turns, wringing out the plush
into my mouth to gag until a gag
no longer worked. The flood stung my ears,
crackling like hymnal leather creased
when I gave my breath and plunged my face
to hold it under, screaming *you stupid bitch*
in little bubbles that always broke
the sun. Each try went longer than before.
You're getting close, I thought the bees might say
as I clawed up, dazed and gasping. Resolved,
I promised I'd stay down and brave the burn
if they kept vigil there, striped like throats
choked amid the shrieks overcome at last
by an engine's growl against the moon
fading into night, still as a body floating.

An Assyrian Eunuch in the Service of Ashurnasirpal II
9th century BC

When they held me down I prayed the dirt
would swallow what they left, no longer boy
but scream, the blade a silver fire swiped
between my legs that burned the blood
it made. When the earth refused to open
I begged fever, the purpled gash, my father
who said my wound would carry us
through palace doors. Halfheartedly
my sisters plied me with their dolls
as if I was a hobbled slave, content
to be their plaything. Somewhere
on the desert road I stopped counting
years. Each day the conqueror
blasts my name down corridors
of Nimrud until my arm again becomes
his wine ladle. In time you'll come
to know the name of childlessness
is honor, the priests all say. When drunk
mighty Ashurnasirpal dribbles
commands into his beard. My silk
wipes them and I nod. I nod
and swat away the summer flies.

Jesse Owens Races a Horse in North Dakota
July 22, 1945

The drunkest fans slosh beer to watch it steam
across the stands. By the bottom of the fifth
it breaks a hundred on the Bismarck field
where players wilt and shuffle off, morose.
The promoter's dented bullhorn gleams:
today his thoroughbred, splendiferous
Prince Martin, makes history. Owen's heels
still ache from racing outfielders whose boast
before the game was they'd take his golds like toys.
Each time he won he hustled silently
back from the dandelion patch to stretch
and go again. No one saw him later retch
behind the dugout. The horse wins easily.
The PA booms *let's hear it for that boy.*

Carousel

in dizzy pony lights I can't recall
how many times around because they smiled
those intermittent faces as I whirled
that seemed so old inside their weariness
their ghosts a decade younger than me now
who perched me on a saddle made of light
to tug the reins that bolted to a jaw
contorted in a frozen open neigh
for every summer orphan's hands that grimed
their manes with popcorn grease or sugar dust
from funnel cakes we tore apart to make
the circle end and overbright the bulbs
rainbowing night so nearby towns would know
whatever joy they spun was incomplete

Tolerance

After eight, my age, I stopped counting
how many beers my father drank
on half-price night. His latest girl tucked
herself under his arm, calling cute
everything the popcorn stench
greased across the fairgrounds—
whack-a-mole, the fishbowls plopped
with ping-pong balls, a Ferris wheel
I rode into the purple sky away
from rumbling generators and neon.
From time to time she'd sneak out
a can to hiss into her hair before
humidity frizzed it down again.
Then the lion I won by drowning
a clown's mouth sat on her shoulders,
their tawny manes tangled. Her laugh
was squeaky even when she stood
in our stoop's shadow, the house keys
locked inside on his firehouse ring.
She twirled there chewing gum
as we straggled around back to find
some strategy between us. His hands
shook like saucers on a train. So I opened
his knife, standing on two palms
that quaked beneath me, to gash
a screen and push the window up
before falling into rooms he won
in the divorce, the rooms he fought to keep.

Neighbor

after Ashley Seitz Kramer

He wants to be unfound, the boy cutting
grass, who is learning to subtract

a bandana from his mangled neck,
pushing hard across the yard's traffic

of flies. When his weak noose snapped
he fell right through magenta,

January's thin snow and the crunch
of both ankles. The story goes he begged

they take that frayed extension cord out
of his allowance. His mother shattered

her rosary leaping in the ambulance.
The parish fed her more. Sometimes

I hear his school friends pummeling
his door. They want to see the scar again.

I need to believe their fingers quake
to feel it, raised and pink. I need to see him

yank the engine, how each row brings
his long bangs back into his face.

The Boy Lincoln

Gangly, neglecting the hogs, he hides
among locust trees two acres out
to scribble maudlin poetry and nap
in larksong, his head having slid
to a trunk's dimple. Thomas Lincoln
bellows *Abe* over the mane
of his stooped mare, startling himself
with the bitterness in its echo. June
drips down his shirtsleeves. He trips
on piles of unsplit wood. How
unmanly, he sighs, this son
who wastes his huge hands borrowing
books that swallow moonlight,
long after snuffed tallows furl
shadows down their one cramped room.
Widowed and starved, neither pretends
to season the corncake they bake
as they peel on dirty bedclothes.
If at night they dream the same
river raft run ashore, its lashed logs
sprayed with silver dollars, at dawn
they say nothing, staring at the glint
of a fork in the other's fist.

Patter

The only sound my father loved was rain
at night, its dark cascade down windowpanes
that washed him into sleep. A boy, I drowned
inside it too and let it charm the count
of empties crowded by the sink that shone
a hazy brown bouquet in nightlight glow.
Sometimes entranced I'd tiptoe out to lick
their mouths, and as I grew, I made them clink
their glass against my teeth to drain their dregs
like drops from dead canteens. What did I dredge
besides the muffled coughs that burned inside
my fist? I'd brace my dizziness, which widened
with the hall, then fall between my football sheets
where men erased the earth beneath their cleats.

Operation Pike, Vietnam, 1967
for Bill Ehrhart

In sleep I drift through fog until the skull
returns—that village newborn's temple burst
like eggshell, rags drenched in mist, his mother's arms
still cradling him though blood spills down her breasts
where shrapnel split her like a rations tin.
What can my stupid ghost absolve for the ghost
morphine makes her there, a dappled moan
that slumps at last to birth her own release?
Bill, all week your book of nightmares pulls me back
to this one page I have no right to name.
I thrash awake and find no better end
for when a body is at last a song
of flies, the pity needle's pinch, a breeze
through hunched Marines who rise and limp away.

July Picnic, Seminary Ridge, Gettysburg

Our toddler peers into the cannon's mouth
and finds green boredom there. The bat's crack
draws him back to uneven teams that lost
the score and laughed, their sandals slipping off
between bases. One daughter makes herself
a maple queen, barely visible high
above the whoops in forking branches gnarled
to weave and wear a leafy sweat-shine crown.
Cantaloupe chunks bleed out for flies that dart
in erratic corkscrew fits, distracting us
from our dream of rain to break humidity.
Giggling, two filthy shirtless boys fence
with foam pool noodles, oblivious
to hunger and the boneyard century
that left its lead to wound the earth they print.
The nearest brigade plaque, so close I could
ping it with a wiffle ball, declares
without punctuation that by nightfall
seven hundred men were unaccounted for.

Public Television

the caught gosling chirps
waning in the vixen's
mouth as six starved kits
crowd insensible leaping

its plump yellow tuft
falls and we zoom in
to see it torn open like a goddess
cursed inside her own fable

summer the Arctic greener
than a ball field the narrator
drifts to the gaggle fleeing
on the quicksilver river

who glide the question marks
of their necks spritzed
and glistening impossible
to tell if this is their grief

or animal amnesia that binds
them shivering as they fade
to clots inside a vein beneath
the glacier's broken teeth

Captive Raptor

for Anna-Lisa Hillenburg

The kestrel clutched our ranger's padded fist,
its rust-streaked cheeks jerking quizzically
from girl to girl. We listened drowsily in mist
before the thunder broke, before we leaned
beneath that tiny canopy to keep
at least our shirtfronts dry. *'Imprinted' means
she can't survive outside captivity,*
the ranger sighed, then continued streaming
through camp. That night I dreamed inside the storm
both girls cawed to help a beak rip out
its handler's eyes, swallowing his warm
and tendrilled nerves. Like Oedipus without
a trail to stagger bleeding on the loam
they flew into the dark to speak with stones.

Dialogue with Dead Mosquito

Did you know your mother?

Fog raised the whirring riverbank.

How did you learn to hunt?

We swallowed the smaller screams.

Who cowered from the dragonflies?

I cheered them faster in the feast.

When did you curse us with itching?

You always oozed your woulds.

Why do we worship summer?

It blinds you with forgetfulness.

Why do we worship flight?

Because your myths are parched.

What is the secret of wings?

Your blood smashed on a wall.

Egging
for Chris Bell

A sidearm lob would splat the oozy crack
we craved, creeping moonlight in second gear,
its haze so faint our runny yolks appeared
to glaze like giant honeyed snails down trunks
of sleeping neighbors' cars. A lob and not
a heave, which early on we learned could thud
so loud a porchlight once behind us blazed
to life and made us floor the night. We'd hit
three stores to buy a dozen each and say
our weary mothers sent us out, too wrecked
from nursing shifts to plan Sunday breakfast.
The lie was mine. In truth I loved it more
than soaring orbs at cars, how one clerk blessed
my teenage heart while creasing my receipt.

A Roman Harlot's Midnight Soliloquy

Nights I drain Caesar into his dream
of blood I cannot sleep. I'm gone
by dawn so he rehearses it

for weeks just to burden me
when I return: the senate burned,
the senate flayed before their sons.

Terraced here above the flickering
candles of an ordinary hush
I see my sisters skitter alleyways

like spiders in an ossuary. We drip
from bed to bed. Our mothers
wept for marriages until coins

sang across their tables. Now
they just mumble kneading bread.
Tomorrow my purse of names

will wear those selfsame shadows
for centurions, who turn boyishly
away when I rise afterwards

to wash. These last palace hours
I'll sip gossamer wine and sweat
my braid to ivy tangled on my back.

I like to feel the wet curls cling.
I like the salt-sweet musk
beneath my arms because it's mine.

Nightie

edamame green and lace the last
August breeze blew through it
like a windsock the idle rich soar
above their beachfront cottage to say
look even the air we own that too

at twelve I was old enough to want it
against my cheek but didn't nor did I
want to see it on my friend's
sister's college body that most
humdrum of boyhood fantasies

no what I wanted was an improbable
lingered flapping on the clothesline
past supper past our bruising vacant
lot touchdowns at sundown to glance
from my window hued by star-frost

and find it there still knuckled
by wooden pins long after the men
of Spring Branch Drive in weariness
drove home greasy hungry ready
to yell away another muggy dusk

I wanted the dishwasher bones
of his mother's hands to drape it
on the porch so I could tiptoe nervously
in dew to clip it high and rightful for
our crooked hours left to stun the moon

Companion Planting
for my wife

Our crippled summer's sunflowers rise up
twenty feet, so cartoonish here above
the rot of cucumber and melon vines
charred like nests of poisoned baby snakes.
At night I smoke my pipe and stare through slate-
gray smoke at maned medallions hovering
shed-high, abob with frowns that seem to find
the ground they've left most worthy of their cupped
stares down. Bamboo-straight, verdant stems will bleed
the Saturday we hack them for the woods.
Our sons will help each other drag the dream
and mighty reach for sky out to our ditch
where wearily I mark each year and pitch
drooped Christmas trees on Boxing Day. Dark green
they'll stain, with petals littered down their hoods.

II

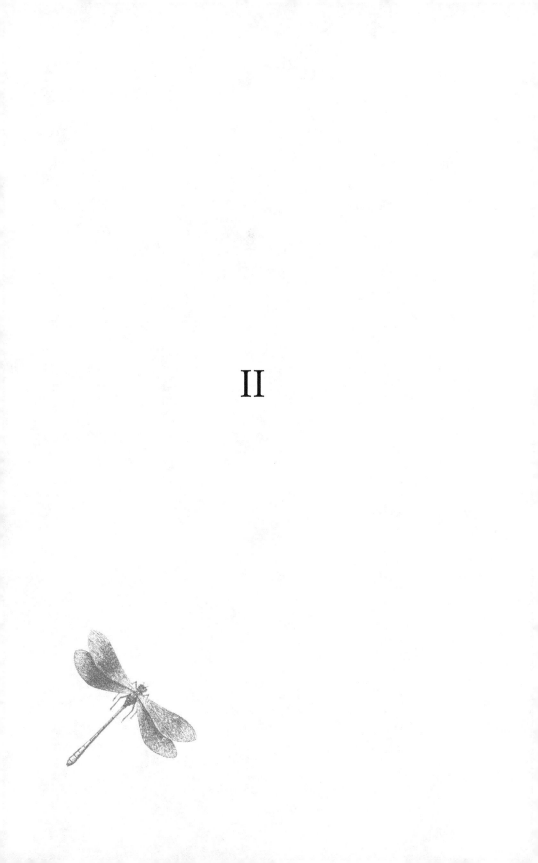

Autumn Scene in Perry County

Mennonite girls at sunset float
across the hill, ringed and giggling.
Their dresses, stiff triangles
blue and cream, scrape wind.
Holding hands, they have no use
for centuries. Snug bonnets
cup bulging buns wound
to their crowns. When the light
changes, I drive past their church,
their unadorned omphalos,
from whence the news
spread like ivy rash that morning
after the farmhouse fire:
seven sisters lay by age
in seven coffins planed by hand.

At the Fairbanks Airport
for Sean Hill

We drove all day and saw no moose, no elk,
no magnificent lumbering from that brush
brisk September turned to shivering
rainbows broken only by the crest
of snow-capped domes, still as sleeping breasts.
Those hills were theirs to roam through after all.

Now my consolation relic of the wild
flashes back from its cage of museum light:
a beaded Athabascan moose-heart bag
resting on a nest of shredded bark.
Clumsy and misshapen as a fetus,
its hollow chamber could have held our hands

plunged wrist-deep. In the snapshot that I took
the glass reflects our faces side by side.
More accurate to say our faces both
are bearded glares. Sean, the terminal's
stale popcorn stench clings to loneliness.
I watch the pulsing planes ascend to tufts

of dingy sunset clouds. The beautiful
couple who let their daughter wander off
ignore her squealing raid through rows of chairs.
She flees our gate to cross the aisle and pet
the husky stuffed atop a sled. He guards
the gift shop's shirts of antler silhouettes.

Still Life with Burn Barrel

Slow rain cascades inside the hollow eyes
a buck's skull upside down stares at the sky,
weeping in reverse—an antlered crown,
gnarled and ochre, my wandering nephews found
and placed atop a woodpile tarp beside
the barrel where we burn. Old receipts glide,
ember-pocked, curling dervishes in heat
that wilt and blaze their figures sheet by sheet.
Above, two wrens confused by smoke resolve
I mean them harm and flee. My boots absolve
a ceramic pot of its remaining shape.
Jagged ostraka, what sentences escape
your angry glow? Your script of roots writhes,
snakelings a widow torches in their hive.

Motel Light

Did she tell us, her sweet illegitimates
bouncing double queens, she ran
this time for good? I don't remember.
Down the corridor I carried moonlight
in an ice bucket, its cold steam swirling
into September. I filled it without asking
each time her gin ran low and sweat
into the nightstand branded with swirls
from other glasses. Drowsy, we clicked
the television knob until we found
a talking horse, that wholesome
absurdity. They smear peanut butter
on its gums, mother mumbled, laughing.
My sister giggled in the same high key.
I didn't care they left the curtains open.
The oily lot flickering, the pool pitiful
as a bedpan were ours and no one's,
unmapped. I sipped the melt's sheen
gone, my mouth against plum smears
of lipstick, and watched until they slept.

Children Sleeping

my mother once said nothing
is more beautiful than the way
children scrunching in a nest
of sheets breathe with the slow
assurance of clouds pajamas
riding up their legs in the slight
whistle-snore of dream if you
linger in the pooling brightness
from the hall it unnerves
everything you cannot stand
there for more than a peck
on the brow a quick fluff
of comforters balled up like hay
so when your creaky tiptoe
midnights down the floorboards
again with yawns to fan
your hand across their hair it is
because somewhere tonight beyond
crickets it's definitive a hobbled
mother claws the rubble back
and melts into the still cherubic
face of her own flesh that will not wake

Painting Toes

Three sons peel socks and fling them down the hall.
Like pups they circle sheepishly around
their mother, who hefts a box of polishes.
The baby squeals and points at neon orange.
With passing clinks, the older two line up
their rainbow schemes and drum their anxious hands across
bottle-tops, humming softly

the one school taunt they know. When I emerged
from basement jams twenty years ago,
sweat-drenched and stoned, my ears still ringing
with an imitation life I thought was mine,
the beer clerk eyed my thumbnails chipping black
and gave my change before he muttered *faggot*.
Most nights I drank the moon away and drove

until the stoplights hazed like finger paints
a kindergartner swirls into the mess
his teacher warned would be ugly mud.
Each dawn a throbbing fire bloomed through blinds
I ached to rise and close. Our eight-year-old
goes last and brushes on each shade himself,
ignoring those who hover at the door

as he straddles the tub to watch them dry.
He blows and fans his feet, but cranes to check
the clock and see the hour falling now
that glooms his face with Sunday night malaise.
Tomorrow's bullies wait, certain as the stones
the mob flung at St. Stephen in their rage,
who bled and blessed them, falling as he prayed.

Napoleon's Lost Letter in Exile
Saint Helena, 1821

Each sunrise is a split horse bleeding
over my fever. I sneeze from room
to moldy room, jailed in slippers.
The English tutor hides my newspapers.

I want to carve a chalice from his skull.
Instead I count my wrinkles
and divide them by the sea. This island
stinks of kelp and British tea.

Like a boy I touch myself in silences
and weep for Josephine. The cavalry
should have rode me down
until my arms were crushed batons.

In sleep I swim a thousand miles
to hear a plowman in Auvergne
serenade the rump flies his mule
can't swish. Son, let me burn

this letter. I pray no blade opens
your throat. Cool nights I close
my windows but still hear waves
mistake themselves for dynasties.

Six Months after the Divorce

My parents didn't want their jeans to touch,
standing on a narrow crooked pier beside
Schoolhouse Pond in October wind, their hands
clutching a spool they couldn't reel back in.

For months my sister begged to fly her kite,
a Christmas gift, its grinning Care Bear perched
askew in dust above her certain rod,
the streamer pocked with bite marks from her rage

when she prowled time-outs for things to wreck.
At last it soared a hundred feet above
our heads, banking hard right, one spreader gone,
the bear a headless belly flapping like

a grocery bag sucked to a box fan's cage.
I decided on my bench to hate them all
and turned away to watch an overcoat
toss tattered clumps of bread to ducks that left

as quickly as they came in rippling glides
like carvings of themselves, expressionless
and still, their heads too green to be believed.
Beyond the sloping bank my mother's car

purred where soon we'd swap our weekend clothes
from trunk to rusted trunk and warm ourselves
by sitting on our palms—a dull exchange
then fifteen minutes overdue. I heard

the snap before the shriek and turned to spot
a fluttered diamond shrink against the sky
so fast it seemed it never was at all,
as if the distant sun-blanched pines were all

we came to see, as long as we ignored
the broken bitter weeping of a girl
and looping leminscates of string that fell,
a silver hair cascading down the rail.

The Lesson for Today
for James

My strings slice finger plaques each time I ache
a chord to show my son he has to press
until the notes ring clear. At ten, it stings
his fingertips, which in a month will slab
with calluses he'll need to riff away
his headphone nights. By then he'll know two frets
by touch, will know that when I sigh and bleed
our lesson ends. Beyond his door I'll rag
my Gibson down and shout above the crunch
to help him find the bridge. But today
we wince in tune and tap our stocking feet
to keep our changes clean. He makes us crank
our knobs to shake the house. We share the curse
to rush the beat that runs inside our hurt.

The Poet Robert Lowell at Age Thirteen

His thirty turtles humped up in a well,
an armored phalanx crushed beneath their shields,
writhe wounded with their final thirst. They're dying
inside September musk, a mockery
of fisted grass littering their shells. The boy
whose uniform is drenched with mud observes
how the nimblest few emerge to claw the heads
that can't. With one foot raised, he still can't reach
inside the basin far enough to net
these bodies that he dropped their final foot.
Weeping, he blows his snot across the moss
and tries to scrape his blackened fingernails
penknife clean. They look like Yankee graves
so rank with age the mold has filled their names.

Fugitive Silence

If I should recall my ruins
what whiskered half-drunk
boy, sparking at the wheel
of his dead lighter, appears
in memory's flickered static?
He puddles globs of spit
on the chapel steps pouting
his only fire now is streetlight,
star-glare, the slatted glow
through dorm blinds where
kegger giggles tumble, echoing
across the dew-damp quad.
He pities himself and lobs
a mushy, half-smoked joint
at shrubs. Let me call him
fledgling, little beak-chirp,
cloud-shadow, fool.
What counterfeit invitations
the reddened leaves make
skittering across his petty
jealousies and gloom.
Inside the church behind him
an organ's silver bones shimmer
faintly, gashing, without music.

John Coltrane at Ground Zero
Hiroshima, 1966

Your translator paced the empty train
until he found you dreaming wide awake,
alone, clacking scales up and down
a tuneless flute that shimmered in your lap.
The city's tidy angles made you grin.

Adamant, you insisted handlers drive
you straight to the memorial where snapshots
freeze you still, hunched and ministerial
laying a wreath, your reverent grief
outlasting the patience of the band.

John, I woke just now to read how a gunman
raged into a Texas church and splintered
pews so he could decimate the cowering
worshippers who shrieked and hugged the floor.
When his rifle crossed a five-year-old

he blasted sunlight through her ribs.
I turned away to fold my toddler's clothes
and scrub flecks of spaghetti sauce
one washing could not undo, praying
the stains come out. Half-awake, I feed

them now into the machine thundering
our half-dark house where three children snore,
each burrowed in a mess of twisted sheets.
This window shields us from an autumn dawn
with clouds ablaze like pentecostal tongues.

Let me turn back. Let me endure the scroll
of faces gone. Let me find the will
to sing a dead child's name into the sky.
Like you I'll lace my hands and squeeze my eyes
and try to make some music from the bomb.

Abel

the cloud said you
are the first riven
bones choose
whichever blue
kingdom of forgetting
for your birthright

I can give the veiled
garden it said
or the throne
of stars you spied
each night sleepily
glimmering above
your dutiful crook
son of ewes

but I refused
saying flocks shall
river over clover
stemming wispily
from my body
in bunches among
this clay oblivion
like mother's
thin hair molded
to her skull

let me raise finally
some bleating
in this wilderness
a chorus rather
than you who are
rainless thunder
not maker but maker
of accomplices

On the Death of an Old Lover

How can I grieve the news your husband found
your body cold across the basement couch
then hid (at least these online rumors say)
the macabre still life of two razored lines
of blow you cut and left? He made the call
I couldn't make. You were unbuttoning
in drunken candlelight our first night
together twenty years ago. Through fog
I see you, sweat-streaked, rise from bed to flip
the record, snort a bump, and straddle me
again. We were too thin. Whose blue uniform
was whose? You draped them both like artifacts
on the desk where my textbook on Pompeii
glossed infants twinned inside a womb of ash.

Playing Dead

for my son Graham

The room shatters with giggles
before your hand's thin worms
burrow my ears. When that fails
they hook inside my cheeks
and nose. Two thumbs pry
my eyelids back—tent flaps
hazing a pink excuse
for morning. When they fall
my name hangs its syllable
on your breath, steadying
beside the final cruelty
a body leaves as its goodbye.

A Nursing Program's Simulation Lab
On the Morning After Graduation

Frozen in their agony, the mannequins
ail in the darkened bay. A wan light falls
from the windowed wall, draping dingy gauze
across thin blue blankets tucked under chins.
Unplugged machines that boast their cost in size
have power cords atop their boxy frames
in coils, like tails the taxidermist blames
for lengths too thin to stuff with his disguise.
Beside each bed, a slender nightstand holds
an empty breakfast tray, a paper cup
for pills, and in a vase, one plastic rose
too perfect in its bloom. Above, tacked up
on boards, the campus daycare's cards are fanned
with trees the children limbed by tracing hands.

Blue Horror

a crush of nurses elbow
their version of the story
down the intensive care
corridor to claw his tongue
back up a narrow well so
I burrow in scratches his
DTs cratered in my palms
to brace against the blue
flashes even in the family
room where one ending is
a breath deep as a gunshot
fired straight inside a field's
dark chest and the other
is some strange hand lightly
grasping my shoulder to pull
me from the meadowhawks
behind my eyelids whirring
unstartled where I dry fire
my revolver at the harvest

Halo Glean

I woke resolved to clean the field of leaves
and peel their colors back to match my grief
until the stubble acreage that reached
beyond horizon's curve possessed the free
furrows of a hand stripped of rings. Their gold
and russet lit my barrow's rust each load.
I cursed the winter sun that fell to kiss
my gap-toothed rake and stragglers I missed
tossing fistfuls on the bonfire. Soon
enough I heard myself accuse the moon
of glowing so shattered stalks looked whole.
And though I pulled it from the sky and broke
its smug halo, some stars still lit the clouds.
All night I wore their ashes for my shroud.

Green Regalia

Just shy five miles our richest neighbor mows
masked with his oxygen. His cheeks spill out
and jiggle when he turns his orange machine
for rows on acres of a lawn so vast
he sometimes rides in rain or dark, his beer
clutched like a torch. I am the sore buffoon
who always waves, jogging away from forty.
One time he gave a reflex shoo. The green
regalia he sprays across our country road
is shy the freedmen's church with all its plaques,
where those of us with ladders keep up the paint.
Where once a boy shaped like his son was seen
with hoods on Halloween, too drunk to burn
green doors they lit and fled, saved by the storm.

III

Mountain Logic

Crossing Sterretts Gap the houses look
like stamps the local suicide tossed in moss
to know the pain of pieces—her scrapbook
nights beneath the sheets, the flashlight's gloss
over each exotic perforation
she disowned in woods behind her house
where once she saw a fallen nation
of robin's eggs spill little suns. She doused
what tears she had but gave up grief for blood
inevitable as the sting her razor nicked
across her wrists. Our mountain logic says
here there is a valley where we can love
the tidy squared-off rows we plow and pick.
Each year we brave the avalanche and stay.

The Blue Daughters of Hotton
December 1944

The night we burned our chairs I blessed the storm
for freezing hands that mortared snow, which slowed
their nearing booms, if only for one pass
of stars. I felt my fever cheeks unwince
as Nora told her dream again: brother back,
a bearded scarecrow, who woke us knocking
on windowpanes before rushing in to scoop
his baby up. Together they spun
buttons off his soldier's coat. I didn't weep
this time to hear it told, to have our dead
come warm the room—confused the phonograph
was gone, how gaunt our Christmas faces were
from want of bread. When gusts struck chimney cracks
we drank their smoke, until the wood ran out.

1987

I clutch the empty plastic tray for globes
my father paws, unlooping from the tree.
Browning needles mist each time he slides
one off and shoves it with a scowl at me.

Alternating the gold and ruby orbs
I crinkle into place, I try to hide
their chipping flakes facedown. The attic heat bakes
their brittle enamel shells, which warp

a little more each year. At five I know
he won't replace them. His whiskey ice
diminishes in clanks, sweating rivulets
that pool before they plunge the mantle's side.

He reaves the heirloom star. I clasp the set.
This is as old as we will ever get.

Morning Jog on Boxing Day

I linger stretching as they drown the elf
who grins at torture in his Christmas suit.
Their other victims, all dolls, drench the shelf
they've made out of a chestnut stump where boots
sucked off by mud lie half-submerged in muck.
Barefoot, soaked, the younger sister stands to roll
baggy pajama bottoms up. She tucks
her shirt and creeps, graceless as a foal
back down beside the creek to fan her hair
inside the ice-shard swirl. My chuckle breaks
the spell—no wave or soft hello can glue
their morning whole again. Both girls glare
before their sprinting feet stamp little lakes.
The cattle fence crackles at beads of dew.

Fox Wake

for Madara Mason

still wronged I think this vixen's bark
on nights of frost I cannot sleep
her throat here in our dying year
quavering acres newly ours
I doze and trace her phantom roam
from woods to fallow pasture weeds
I'll never till to plant but mowed
in raw July when my sneakers squished
with sweat as sunburnt I climbed down
to touch the bushy eyebrow of
her fur intact no blood the mouth
agape the razor pearls of teeth
her legs outstretched and sprinting in
the dirt what unseen wound she kept
through shovelfuls I cursed to make
her disappear and now such yowls
their desperate searching vacancies
have come starlit to beg back bones
to pant one final hunt and claim
the only body she could dare
consumed beyond a gown of flame

Ode to Tissue

O little sail, how quickly you become
a pocket's wad or rumpled cloud inside
the corner of a purse. You get one glance
across a runny playground nose, one daub
of graveyard tears and then we crush you up
as waste, our intimate embarrassment.
Perhaps there is some dignity at least
in being passed, pristine still, in your box
pastiched with tulips, to soften a blow:
I'll help you leave him. We can bury
her dog tags. You have six months or less.
Perhaps there is some puny majesty
with new couples, nervous, panting in the glow,
who pluck you for the aftermath of love.
My friend's son, who stays a boy who's trapped
inside the body of a man, who closes
his eyes every other morning when a hand
that is not his shaves stubble from his face,
knows enough to hide the evidence of night.
My friend doesn't mind you, tissue, balled
and tossed beneath a bed. Each weekend when
he crawls to clean, he finds you light as light,
still bright past damaging, like the body
of the baby wren a cat left on my stoop.
To spare my sons I mummied it in you.
In our darkened woods you matched the snow
and hid for me the bankruptcy of flight.

Husk

Their bodies Byzantine and light as lint,
the wispy dragonflies that died beneath
my hood inside a shallow scuttle drain
were mating still. I found them having fought
to change a battery that wouldn't start,
two knuckles bloodying my ratchet. I swore
at winter's sunset drizzle-chill until
they fluttered counterfeit, a ruse of breeze,
as if May awakened in their antennae
and roused them to their urge. They rasped my skin
the long walk to the pond, my flannel soaked,
and whirled an S of gold each time the storm
broke in my hands. Like a boy I turned before
they sank, two skimmers reddened on the wing.

Footage from the Hide

The mother snowy owl crucifies herself
on wind that rips across the tundra grass.
Her smallest one, delirious and starved,
shivers thick gray down balled on its back,
its tiny heart a marble wrapped in lint.
Beyond, its father swoops for lemming pups
oblivious a shadow creeps across
their own. Rigid as a crossbow frame,
he pitches through a sky inseparable
from the still horizon sea, both steel-blue.
The owlet's lungs flutter and seize between
its mother's feet. We meet the vacant gaze
of grief that lifts a blood-soaked beak that breaks
a child apart for other children's mouths.

Fable

A father pins his son against a wall
and wraps his hand around that little throat
to squeeze it only once, as if to say
I cannot take this wildness of your wings.
An hour afterwards, he wipes a cloth
across the stinging eyes his boy can't close
enough, the soapy rivulets a burn
that rinses with the ducky song they make
together out of time. In thirty years
looped tubes and wires of the ICU
will worm the father's bed. His son will hum
until the nurses flutter off like wrens,
until a final thirst surrenders light
like feathers fanned across the star-burned ice.

Leaving Assateague Island

Our damp feet stamped exclamation points
across boardwalk planks. In dribble
from a shower head calcified and pocked
by salt air, we rinsed Labor Day
off our legs and watched it splotch
in muddy clumps through slats, down
to dunes below. We limped, hefting
the aftermath of castles in mesh bags,
our burned skin tightening in shore breeze.

Chair wefts slackened as we slung them
into the trunk, where a dim bulb
shadowed orange rust ochre on their frames.
When I slammed it shut I saw the halo
blazing a blood-soaked Christ who stormed
a rapture flyer some soul slid beneath
our wiper. It joined a hundred others, skittering
like crabs toward a wild pony, studded
with burrs, plopping golden stones on the lot.

In December, in a white dawn obscured
by plumes of gray exhaust, I popped
the lid, groping for the scraper half-awake.
Sand flecks fell from its handle
into the lopsided angels I scolded
my sons for making by the driveway,
though I stood there, a frigid grin,
coaxing them to swing their arms before
I stooped to pull them from their wings.

Apastron

The day a father dies December snow
falls merciless and clean. His boy of twelve
creates an impromptu shrine before shelves
of records fraying at their seams. He blows
between the sides small asteroids of dust
that accumulate on the stylus tip.
And so begins a wordlessness that flips
dusk to stars, a mom to trembling that must
steady and scrape a plate gone cold away.
She leaves him orbiting to leave the world
and make her soundless shrieks in bed, curled
inside a faded robe that cauls her face.
Hazy amber dials glow against the black.
A shadow fumbles for the headphone jack.

Lee Morgan Nods Off

He is not there, inside the burning head
drenched in steam, slumped on radiator coils
that singe his hair to stench, skin to scar,
a furrowed acreage in drought above
flaxen stains that constellate his undershirt,
not the motel chair beside a window where
a snow-globe Philadelphia keeps track
of every taxi's soundless creep through slush
and scarlet neon ransoms night, bloodying
each parking meter's crown, not the needle,
not the spoon, not the blackened army
shriveled matches make across his lap,
his ashen knees, not in sock garters rigged
with safety pins, his knotted feet, the tray
where cigarette butts bob in day-old milk
or further back, let's sharpen focus there,
the silver horn inside its case upright
upon the bed, what convenient ghost
that brass machine, where even now some spit
in droplets pools beneath the valves, O lord
this room, this rat-trap tomb is vacant still
a moment more until the hanger knifing
its crooked dangle on the closet knob
will shiver from his resurrection wail.

Dear Reader

For all I know, you hate the squeak of shoes
across your kitchen tile, the nervous way
I clear my throat when conversations turn
to wine, or just the sight of ponytails
on men whose temples gray. I have no clue
what you can't forgive. Your window frames
a different smidge of earth. Sometimes I yearn
to sing the birthday song into a wail
but mime my tuneless lips instead. Silence
makes a melody of awkward air
that later blows the candles out. My gift
is a small token wrapped hysterically
with the obituary page. If you sift
you'll find the one who clutched at sirens.

Road Flares

They sizzled red like cartoon dynamite—
four incandescent sticks that marked the wreck.
They sparked on shards of sleet, as if a prince
had smashed his brandy at the candlelight
on hearing that the maid he favored last
had sank into a pond to drown the shame
two moons had made. I braked, but passed too fast,
and had to merge, to catch more than a glimpse—
one desperate pump above the driver's breasts.
Three EMTs, all young enough to be
my sons, were blurs. They may have winced, crackling
through walkie-talkie static to relay
she's gone. Who knows. I dropped a gear to see
one pumper's thrust, the steam rise off his back.

My Father's Truck

His rear-view mirror dangles like a claw
that tore on prey that was no prey at all
but mouse-round stone. A stack of circulars
addressed to neighbors yellow on the floor.
A moldy liquor box slashed down its side
spills clothes (some tagged) he never wore. Behind
that, farther still, shadows read the cast
of bills where every notice was the last.
A hundred Miller cans, crushed and lusterless
as broken stars, poke through bags. *Hiss hiss*
is what escapes when I crank up the heat.
Inside, a landlord disinfects the seat
where my father clutched the dark and fell.
Come back, O ghost, and drive us from your hell.

For a Crash Test Dummy

The techs who propped your hands at ten and two
have given us the grim appearance
of suicide. You coast slow-mo inside
your blank sedan, a turtle shell that glides
downstream pristine, an adolescent thing,
the aftermath of hawks who swooped to rip
its plated belly out. Your chrome trim gleams
in filming light. Two child seats in the back
belt in the air, their plush cushions plump,
having never held an infant's thrash or puke.
Ahead, an erected stack of bricks
juts up six feet from the laboratory floor
like some excavated fortress wall
comically incomplete, its last defense
a platonic rectangle that protects
its shadow from the sun. Beige and hairless,
your narrow, stickered head wobbles, wearing
an unblinking servant's grin. Milliseconds
tick up the counter, which freezes when we see
without the thin dignity of clothes
your bloodless body blooming through the glass.

Skull Winter

The hill we called a mountain froze
a sheer sheet the blizzard's second day
when wind blew powdery beards
on maple trunks. Panting to the top
in pity boots that almost fit I smirked

each time I caught a glimpse beyond
of our school convent, desolate
as a dead calf's barn stall,
where those bitter sisters were left
to scold themselves. My older cousins

squealed, zipping down in puffs of ice
so far below at times I couldn't tell
who among us steered so brazenly
toward the apple tree, just to jerk
before the crash, then roll, crunching

to a stop. Heaving, they each laid
puffy as a sleeping bag, the remnant
storm whipping red cheeks redder.
The rusty sled that fell to me
would hardly turn. Baling twine

mottled as oatmeal soaked up slush,
slackening around planks as hours
wore on, until at last I aimed
my crossbow peak at branches
and lurched. I wish when I awoke

I was glad to see the faces
of kin encircling me, teary
and relieved, a sky featureless
as slate and the boyish glory
of a sled in splinters. But I shut

my eyes again to the commands
to count their show of hands, aching
with a strange new grief I was
called back from the silence there
inside the bark, ringed and endless.

Apocryphal

What could we do? Their drunken father sawed
his cypresses and groveled at the clouds
that growled their booms. His ragged greasy beard
frayed from his chin in clumps, just like a goat's.
We watched his sons grow thin upon their hill
and marveled at the nights his tears became
their only meal. The other shepherds jeered
what kind of prophet gives his heart to doom,
then flocked across his curse. We came to loathe
the ark and wished his wife, though bruised, would ply
her wine then stab him in his sleep. Most gods
are noise. The ravens scattered off on dawns
he hammered sky. At last we held his dream
beneath the surf to burn each gasp that blued.

Origin Story

My mother, a young nun, begged the waterfall
to thunder her guilt to gasping. I was told
her face was beautiful when a friar pulled it
marbled from the foam. The sweet antiquist
who raised me in the spire's shadow dealt
best in dinettes. Our attic's jumbled banquet
was a feast of dust. I was my only guest
with stocking puppets on my hands. Later
whenever I shivered errands the village
studied me like Ecclesiastes. I resembled
the fathers most devout. Whenever I built
a blanket ark on nights I couldn't sleep
I paired the stars for beasts but left the moon
alone, milky through my pinhole frays,
her face too pale and tortured to be loved.

IV

Garden Glass

Because it's what they'd always done
the old couple who owned this house
before we bought it from their son
would limp their trash beyond grass
and bury it among the roots
beneath a maple canopy
that still was yard but mostly dirt:

a spot where only sun-streaks peeked
in pinhole shafts that barely lit
the worms that inched the rubber bands
their bodies made, spelunking junk.
That spring we had the energy
of childless newlyweds and trimmed
those branches clear. Excitedly

we thought our spades, which bore the pale
tattoos where clearance stickers
were thumbnailed off, could excavate
the thousand flakes of Styrofoam,
the crescent wrenches rusted tight
as jaws of feral dogs that froze,
and endless glass, rainbowing

umber, cerulean, and mint.
I would wheel the barrow over
so we could clink its shiny mouth
with jagged trapezoids that snagged
our cotton gloves. After showering
we lay in bed and traded wounds
against the night. A decade later,

each heavy springtime rain reveals
the fragments of our vanity
emerging still in rows of beans.
After storms sputter from the stars
it looks by dawn as if the earth
has wriggled from a bridal gown
to flash her belly scars in sun.

Planet Earth in Reverse

The wolf unclamps his jaw
from a bison's shredded flank.
Spritzes of blood mid-air
stream back inside the wound
snapping shut like a gill.
They slalom backwards
through glassy boulders
and sheets of snow-crust
furrowed as a miner's palm.
The calf dissolves into a herd
that wends its question mark
around a lake of steel. Raised
atop his ridge, the wolf
droops his pert ears when
the last brown tuft meanders
out of view. And so he too
retreats the scented miles until
his certainty returns to hunch,
then whim, then unburned air
outside his den. There, his hunger
recedes to rib-thin sleep,
a commercial break, a lurch in time.
Runt again, he feeds the teat
dribbled yellow milk
unraveling from snout fur.
Dawn fades back to blackened
cloud-creep. Puffed and plump,
the pup wriggles deeper
into a dark river of brothers.

Cain

the truth is that I never loved
the land this dirt communion
my father's blackened fingernails
desperate cupping blossoms
his lips babbled out of names

each day he tracks the sun
and like a blind runt loses
himself winced shivering
sore hands twitching broth
to his mouth in firelight

given to wrinkles mother
a hag a sag of rags impossible
to remember her bone-smooth
body rising from the swirl herself
a garden soft as twilight once

I stalked into sky and found
only sky nothing
ancient booming mountainous
nothing huddled behind clouds
to beg or bless or pardon

wilderness is the courage yes
to say brother let us go
see our true faces in the river
and strike until his blood
ripens my broken stone

Murder Show Bingo

Fade in. Trailer park. A Firebird
peeling paint like skin three days
after sunburn. Reenactment cast
with better teeth than anyone
in the real family photos. The phrase
wanted a better life. Awkward
commercial break. Job at gas station.
Job at bowling alley. Job tending bar.
A white man in jeans proving quickly
he isn't human. Long panning shot
of a hatchet and duct tape shown
twice. Wine glass smashing
in slow-mo. A dolled-up neighbor
who can't form sentences quaking
before she sobs. The word *ligature*.
Behind the headboard, one fleck
of blood. Lead detective
retired. Lead detective dead
from cancer and 87 crime scenes
in his head. An aunt moping through
faded birthdays in a shoebox
to help producers milk the hour.
Near the end, blue gloves taking
underwear from an evidence bag
to show the camera how plain
they are, like ours, and stained.

Listing

Come see our siding glimmer in the sun.
Our knuckles stung in bleach. All cobwebs gone.
Come see our daffodils like little gods,
these yellow resurrections born to nod
again in April breeze. Our vase-staged rooms
are dustless as a baron's desk. We groomed
them free of poetry (my books in bins
teeter attic stacks) and snapshots of our kids
the realtor said to hide. Come see the crack
my son punched in the wall. The spackle
filled the dent but couldn't fix it all.
Come see the bed where we make love. We fall
like peasants to our sleep. Some moons I grind
but nothing's cursed. The nightmares are all mine.

1946

I hung the year again, my neighbor said,
pointing at her tacked yellowed calendar,
because I wanted Harold to remember
seeing those green galoshes frozen
like fossils in the ice of Dennis Creek.
That was the only March he ever tried
to bake my birthday cake. When it sank
he limped down to Wilkinson's and bought
five pies. By May his army cane stayed
dusty in our umbrella bin. Sundays
after mass we picnicked with the Murrays
who whistled Glenn Miller melodies.
By late summer I was pregnant
with Jeanie but didn't know it yet.
Harold built the shop out back himself.
He always had one purple fingernail.
Evenings I'd hang wash and curse
his burn pile. We swapped crosswords
listening to crickets on the patio
and symphonies from our Farnsworth.
On the anniversary of Hiroshima
I found him clothed and rocking
in the tub. When I yanked the kerchief
from his teeth he sobbed
Delila help me wash these ashes off.

Sympathetic Magic

Exhaustion saw a falcon in the unraveling swaddle
her arms swayed. Hush. Hack. The microwave clock
pooled an aquamarine haze across linoleum
sticky from the dropper's last dribbled dose.
I'm going to lay this boy back in his bassinet,
she thought, leave the front door open, and they'll find

my slippers in the train yard—slippers and a tooth
blasted thirty yards away, nestled like a shard
of eggshell April breezes blew in crabgrass.
The apartment rattled like a serving tray
when freight cars rumbled by, eight minutes
past every hour. Instead she rubbed her thumb

on gums quivering between wails, which flared
more wails, made blanket folds akimbo feathers
silvering darkness. At last she stole a sand dollar
from the mantle, swiped its dust across her robe,
and spun its edge into wounding until sunlight
pierced through curtains gapped like parted lips.

What They Roared

You whore. I'll take the kids. Don't let the door
slam on your ass. Because I called the bank.
You're drunk again. You scrub it then. Those clowns
you call your friends are dicks. I'll smash this bowl
of flakes upside your head. Who cares I winked?
Because you're fat. I'm done. Your mother's calls
are hell. Get out. Drop dead. You first. Just shut
your goddamn mouth. If I could get it off
I'd throw this ring into the sea. I hope
your lawyer's good. I'm going to smash this car
and all your bullshit tears into a tree.
You shaved for me? I love that dress. Let's go
the sitter's here. The rain just stopped. These lilies
smell heavenly. It's time to eat. I'm home.

Plague

The decadent amazement didn't last.
Sure, at first I hugged bystanders in the rain,
quaking dumbstruck at the oak I missed a yard
away, my truck on its side, a crushed can
of soup. When someone said an angel
led me crawling out to rise unscathed and pour
glass from my boots, I wept. But three days
later, my stiffness left. The belt's red snake
that burned diagonally across my chest
faded with the spring. In honors history
I wrote my final essay on the plague.
The few who fevered to survive broke
quarantine to aid kerchiefed priests, then strolled
immune down poisoned streets to rob the dead.

Pieta

She's famous still, a local god, the girl
who yanked a Chevy above her waist
just high enough, a shriek three seconds long,

until her father freed the mangled hose
his leg became, scarleting the grass.
At eight she had the wherewithal to call

and give the dispatcher her address
before she slammed inside the screen to fetch
a towel to wrap the gore. She never named

the song she hummed against his glaucous lips
that faded into kisses for two temples
rag-dolled in her lap. The Catholic fireman

first on the scene would later say he shut
his siren off before the farm to spare
them all the noise—his migraine, barbwire cows,

and the farmer's tiny child he thought
he'd find but didn't find, discovering instead
a bent Madonna, tearless in the hush.

Faking It

A dug-up corpse could wear your favorite shirt
face-down on the gorge's scrubby floor beside
the burning s'more your flipped car made. That used
to be enough to make the world believe
you stomped your brakes but plummeted the blur
of crags that whipping past tore out your scream.
The coroner would cringe and nod. Your aunt
twice divorced would take the pooch. College friends
would snivel, leaking on the casket lid.
Older now, they'd need some wine to bag
your apartment up. Two states away, you'd spin
and try on shades inside the minimart.
How gleaming each could look with butchered hair,
your dye rinsed down a motel drain like phlegm.

Barabbas on His Deathbed

Some nights I mocked the night, a walking stick
across my shoulder blades, just drunk enough
to revel in the brothel stench. I'd ply
the youngest girls disgusted by my scars,
delighted by their shuddering. Too gruff,
one madam nagged, even as she counted up
my gleam from smuggling. Reborn, I licked
the mutton fat clean off my fingertips.
This Rome's a mouth that dreams its hungers far
beyond the sea—we've lain like wine-dazed fauns
and fed each other grapes. That carpenter
sang out for nails. My slave, when I'm all coughs,
prays to his Christ. Of course, he'll rob the dust
and what it hides the morning I don't rise.

A Convalescent Bed in a Field of Yellow Tulips
for Daniel Lawless

Your wires trail into a gopher hole.
A tea of clover greens the IV bag.
Two mice have made the stack of pillows propped
their soft cathedral. They scratch like children
impatient for a homily to end.
Frost fans its ragged ponytail across
the footboard. No spiders creep the sheets.
It seems a stretch, but you can yawn and push
the comforter into a little mound
of springtime snow so a cardinal can land,
resplendent as a sore, to peck and pull
holly berries from your socks. His sleek
and pointed helmet finds its feast. He's come
to beak each reddened host upon your tongue.

Revising the Waiting Room Sign

No food. No drink. No forlorn sighs
that let us know you long to be
immune to coughing fits like all
these other weary donkeys come
in gloom to slouch and yawn corralled.
Peruse the yachting magazines
fanned out, their mailing labels snipped
to let a little color bleed
into the sea. Of course you know
the doc's address was there, a square
not far from yours, but huger, dreamed
in a gazebo neighborhood
where walkway lights adorn the mums
at night and make each fresh-cut shrub
glow blue like corkscrewed souls. No need
to squirm. No room has emptied yet
of whispered animosities.
Just count the bricks and chew your nails.
The door will open like a purse.

My Grandfather's Light

after treatments when I'm bleeding
from plaques silvering my kneecaps
I wonder how his raw shins flaked
when he winced shucking
overalls in the basement corner
because no one can remember
how a body burned as it swam
its weightless glisten in the salt
only a foggy childhood strangeness
my aunts and mother conjure
of his ultraviolet lamp nestled
in cobwebs freakish skeletal
like a dead dream's prototype
like a coatrack on a boy's coffin
and the sound it made upstairs
where after dishes there was briefly
a breath eight daughters held
when the floor begat its hum

In the Neurology Wing of Johns Hopkins Outpatient Center

for my son James

The boy with his shattered skull stitched
runs his fingers over the bridge
Van Gogh's rainbow impasto arcs

across the Arles. Water ripples
away from washerwomen stooped,
amorphous, scrubbing on the shore.

Hung beside the receptionist,
the print quakes from the steady thud
a woman knocks with her helmet.

She bangs her wince into the wall
to drown the child inside her moan.
We terrible hosannas tick

our turns to take the corridor.
River of squeaks, river of doors,
a wheelchair's grease streaks down the floor.

Above his jigsaw crown, in spring's
sumptuous light, the boy's shirtsleeve
swirls golden cattails out of dust.

Volunteer Day at Little League Park

The bottle caps and shafts of broken sporks
mound up beside deadfall branches thrown
in clumsy piles. Faint squeaks of rolling paint
emboldening each sun-blanched dugout wall
carry on the gusts that scatter all
the pine needles we've raked. Our tarps, like gowns
clotheslined in a storm, refuse to faint.
And here we are, the stoners, jocks, and dorks
of yesteryear, aligned at last, graying
beneath our hats and hoods. The season calls
us back, inching under bleachers on our knees
to gather up the hot dog foil and balls
last year's ghosts fouled away in weeds. We stay
until the plot of earth we fenced is clean.

An Abandoned Fort in the Woods

the rotted dream of captives
its slant roof littered with acorns
wears the hiked light of Saturday
and spring's last courtesy to frost

if we asked the son who nailed it
his ghost squealing still behind
moss-trunks green as river-skin
green as his bent bike archived

in the gully's bright museum
of cabinets sinks and shower-heads
that once functioned with an ugliness
his parents labored to unmake

would he say the beams crumbled
even on the day he framed them
their discards square enough
one pure campaign of summer

would he say his cousin prisoners
were kindly lodged and hummed
until an aunt's voice echoing hills
arose to break the latch

On What Would Have Been My Father's 65th Birthday

Minnows scrawl cold hieroglyphs
across my feet. Invader, I enter
their stream, having come to rinse
hike sweat in this glassy burble,

a postcard serenity. Father,
I crouch and splash, remembering
how ashamed I was to ask,
and the insistence of the undertaker

that someone identify your body.
When he wheeled you out, cocooned
in sheets, your scalp turbaned
with a towel, I admired the farcical

concealment of an autopsy.
The stream quivers its silver skin.
Your pale, unmade face was one
of these stones, whiskered with moss.

I have carried your lesson here,
inside the mountain's thousand greens
so I may try to refuse
the uselessness of awe.

Acknowledgements

Thanks are due to the editors of the following journals where these poems first appeared, sometimes in earlier versions:

The Arkansas International: "1946"
Asheville Poetry Review: "The Boy Lincoln"
Atlanta Review: "Leaving Assateague Island"
Big Muddy: "Volunteer Day at Little League Park"
Borderlands: Texas Poetry Review: "Mountain Logic"
The Chattahoochee Review: "Dialogue with Dead Mosquito,"
    "For a Crash Test Dummy"
Cherry Tree: "Painting Toes"
Clackamas Literary Review: "Six Months After the Divorce"
Cream City Review: "Children Sleeping"
Diagram: "Revising the Waiting Room Sign"
Diode: "At the Fairbanks Airport," "The Blue Daughters of
    Hotton," "An Abandoned Fort in the Woods"
Ethel: "My Grandfather's Light"
Fledgling Rag: "1987"
Folio: "Murder Show Bingo"
Freshwater Review: "Apocryphal," "Barabbas on his Deathbed"
Gargoyle: "How to Write a Nature Poem"
Glassworks: "Road Flares"
The Georgia Review: "Jesse Owens Races a Horse in North Dakota"
The Gettysburg Review: "Plague"
The Indianapolis Review: "Motel Light"
Innisfree Poetry Journal: "Operation Pike, Vietnam, 1967"
Iron Horse Literary Review: "On the Death of an Old Lover"
Kestrel: "John Coltrane at Ground Zero"
The Little Patuxent Review: "Autumn Scene in Perry County"
Maryland Literary Review: "Faking It"
The Manchester Review: "Cain"

The Massachusetts Review: "The Poet Robert Lowell at Age Thirteen"

The McNeese Review: "Nightie," "Skull Winter"

The Meadow: "Halo Glean"

The Midwest Quarterly: "A Roman Harlot's Midnight Soliloquy," "Napoleon's Lost Letter in Exile"

The Minnesota Review: "Vigil"

The Moth: "What They Roared"

New Plains Review: "Dear Reader"

New Welsh Review: "*Planet Earth* in Reverse"

The Night Heron Barks: "Carousel," "Pieta"

Ninth Letter: "Neighbor"

The Northern Virginia Review: "July Picnic, Seminary Ridge, Gettysburg"

Oxford Poetry: "Footage from the Hide"

Plainsongs: "Public Television"

Ploughshares: "Listing"

Plume: "A Convalescent Bed in a Field of Yellow Tulips"

Poet Lore: "Garden Glass"

Puerto del Sol: "Fable," "On What Would Have Been My Father's 65th Birthday"

RHINO: "Lee Morgan Nods Off"

Salamander: "Playing Dead"

Santa Ana River Review: "Captive Raptor"

Sixth Finch: "Bloom"

Southern Indiana Review: "Tolerance"

Southwest Review: "Companion Planting"

Stirring: "Sympathetic Magic"

St. Katherine Review: "Sympathetic Magic"

Tampa Review: "My Father's Truck"

Third Coast: "Still Life with Burn Barrel"

32 Poems: "Egging," "Fugitive Silence," "Ode to Tissue"

Tinderbox Poetry Journal: "Morning Jog on Boxing Day"

Thrush: "Blue Horror"

Valparaiso Poetry Review: "Patter," "Apastron"

The Westchester Review: "A Nursing Program's Simulation Lab on the Morning After Graduation"

Western Humanities Review: "Husk," "Origin Story"

Willow Springs: "An Assyrian Eunuch in the Service of Ashurnasirpal II"

"The Lesson for Today" originally appeared in the anthology *This Is What America Looks Like* (Washington Writers' Publishing House, 2021).

"Autumn Scene in Perry County" and "Still Life with Burn Barrel" also featured on *Verse Daily.*

I'm also grateful to William Hathaway, who first read these poems and whose insights proved invaluable. The greatest thanks are due to my family: Ann, James, Graham, and Roan.

About the Author

Adam Tavel is the author of four previous books of poetry, including the forthcoming *Sum Ledger* (Measure Press, 2022). His most recent collection, *Catafalque*, won the Richard Wilbur Award (University of Evansville Press, 2018). His recent poems appear, or will soon appear, in *North American Review, Ploughshares, The Georgia Review, Beloit Poetry Journal, Ninth Letter, The Massachusetts Review, Copper Nickel,* and *Western Humanities Review*, among others. He teaches at Wor-Wic Community College, where he also directs the Echoes & Visions Reading Series. You can find him online at http://adamtavel.com/

CPSIA information can be obtained
at www.ICGtesting.com
Printed in the USA
LVHW050540190322
713645LV00004B/16

9 781622 882328